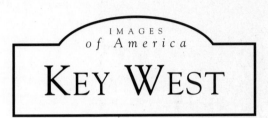

IMAGES
of America

KEY WEST

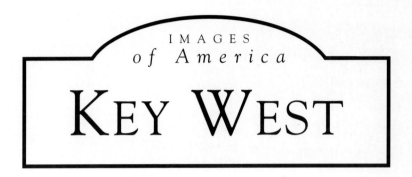

IMAGES
of America
KEY WEST

Lynn M. Homan and Thomas Reilly

ARCADIA

Published by Arcadia Publishing,
an imprint of Tempus Publishing, Inc.
2 Cumberland Street
Charleston, SC 29401

Printed in Great Britain.

Library of Congress Catalog Card Number: 00-108557

For all general information contact Arcadia Publishing at:
Telephone 843-853-2070
Fax 843-853-0044
E-Mail sales@arcadiapublishing.com

For customer service and orders:
Toll-Free 1-888-313-2665

Visit us on the internet at http://www.arcadiapublishing.com

This aerial view of Key West gives an idea of exactly how many structures can be packed onto an island that is only 2 miles by 4 miles in size. The southernmost point in the continental United States, Key West is actually located closer to Cuba than it is to the Florida mainland. In spirit, however, Key West is an entity unto itself. (Key West Art and Historical Society.)

CONTENTS

ACKNOWLEDGMENTS

Many people played a part in bringing this book to fruition. When the Florida Humanities Council sent us to Key West to lecture on Florida's aviation history, we were given the opportunity to realize what a wonderful subject for a book Key West would be. At Arcadia Publishing, Acquisitions Editor Christine Riley and Sales Manager Kate Everingham were quick to share our vision. Executive Director Claudia Pennington and her staff members Gerri Sidoti and Shelley Malone took time from busy schedules to provide us with access to the archival collections of the Key West Museum of Art and History at the Custom House. Shelley also offered us a cherished family photo of her mother as Miss Highway 1928. Tom Hambright generously shared with us his wealth of knowledge, along with the treasure trove of images and information that reside within the local history collection at the Monroe County Public Library. At Courtney's Place, Linda, Danni, and Courtney not only did everything possible to ensure a pleasurable stay, but also provided images of special events. Carol and Ed Swanick allowed us to vicariously enjoy their trip to the Dry Tortugas. Peter Anderson enlightened us about the Conch Republic. And last but not least, Everett and Fredda Glover interrupted their honeymoon to share special photographs that would help us to tell our story.

INTRODUCTION

Ever since its documented discovery by Europeans, Key West has been known by many different names. Spanish explorer Ponce de Leon and his crew named the tiny island Los Martires, or "the martyrs," in 1513. They were by no means, however, the first visitors to the area. Beginning as early as 800 A.D., groups of Native Americans, including Calusas, Matecumbes, Tequestas, and later, Seminoles, had populated many of the more than 800 islands extending southward from the mainland of Florida. Sometime in the 18th century, warring tribes are believed to have fought several pitched battles on the southernmost island, resulting in the death of hundreds. When their dried and bleached bones were discovered years later, the 2-by-4-mile piece of coral received the Spanish name Cayo Hueso, translated as Bone Key or Island of Bones. When the group of islands were ceded to Great Britain, the Anglicized version of Cayo Hueso became Key West.

The island that would come to be known as Key West has had almost as many assertions of ownership as it has had different names. Juan Ponce de Leon gave Spain its claim in 1513. Considered to be of little value, the small chunk of coral became an English possession in 1763, only to return to Spanish control 20 years later. Still known by its somewhat forbidding name of Bone Island, Key West again changed ownership in 1815 when it was given to a Spanish officer, Juan Pablo Salas, as a reward for meritorious service to the King of Spain. Spain ceded Florida to the Americans in 1819; the United States officially took possession two years later. Colonization of the Keys began in earnest.

At the end of 1821, John W. Simonton, an American businessman, purchased Juan Pablo Salas' land for the grand sum of $2,000. He then divided the island into four sections, selling off three of the pieces of property. Representatives of the federal government quickly followed the pioneering settlers. Arriving aboard the U.S. Navy vessel *Shark*, Lieutenant Matthew C. Perry claimed the islands for the United States. Under the American flag, Key West flourished; the community was incorporated in 1828.

The coming years witnessed a population explosion, turning Key West into a true melting pot. Newcomers from the Bahamas, many of English extraction and relatives of Tory sympathizers who had emigrated during the American Revolution, arrived in large numbers during the 1830s. Settlers from southern, eastern, and New England states established homesteads. Blacks, both slave and free, came from the states as well as the West Indies. During the late 1860s, thousands of Cubans fled a revolution in their homeland. Their relocation to Key West expanded an already existing cigar industry and led to an increasingly important

7

social and political role. Military actions, including the Civil War, the Spanish-American War, World War I, and World War II, brought an influx of personnel to Key West.

Fishing, turtling, wrecking and salvage, sponging, making cigars, processing salt, housing the military, and even smuggling were all endeavors that at one time allowed Key West to boast of being the wealthiest city in Florida, if not all of the United States. Unfortunately, forces both natural and manmade conspired to erode much of the city's industrial base. The salt industry succumbed to the combined effects of the Civil War and a hurricane in 1876. Storms at sea drove ships aground on the coral reefs surrounding the Keys, giving rise to the island's wrecking or salvage industry. This proved highly lucrative until lighthouses, lightboats, rescue stations, and other advances in marine safety eventually curtailed the profits. Military influence in the city expanded and contracted with the political circumstances of the nation. During wartime, Key West was an important installation; in peacetime, the military presence declined dramatically.

Mother Nature frequently proved to be destructive—when storms and hurricanes came ashore, they caused loss of life, property damage, and in 1935, the destruction of the railroad. A disastrous fire in 1886 destroyed much of the city, including homes, businesses, and factories. Labor strikes a few years later led to the cigar industry's relocation to Tampa. Key West had been known as the "sponging capital of the world" until a fungus in the sponge beds wiped out an industry that had employed hundreds.

One of the events that would have a profound impact on the community was the construction of the Key West Extension of the Florida East Coast Railway, owned by multi-millionaire Henry Morrison Flagler. In distance, the trip wasn't very far, only 128 miles from Homestead to Key West. The route spanned 42 stretches of open water, with 17 miles of viaducts and concrete-and-steel bridges, and 20 miles of causeways built upon fill dredged from the ocean bottom. In reality, however, the journey had taken years. Although viewed by many as a miracle, Flagler had always known that this marvelous mechanical feat was a possibility.

January 22, 1912, was a proud day for Henry Flagler and the people of Key West, as *Extension Special* pulled into Key West. Flagler's private car, *Rambler*, sat at the end of the train made up of an engine, tender, and five passenger cars. The small island, over a hundred miles from the Florida mainland and formerly accessible only by ship, could now be reached by rail in only a few hours. The crowds were tremendous. Almost everyone living in Key West had turned out for the arrival of what was being trumpeted as "The Eighth Wonder of the World." As the elderly, nearly blind Flagler addressed the welcoming committee, he said, "We have been trying to anchor Key West to the mainland . . . and anchor it we have done."

Key West had indeed been anchored to the mainland, but the cost had been high. The strain of building the railroad had been hard on the 82-year-old Flagler; he died the next year. One of the founders of the Standard Oil Company, Flagler had purchased a railroad from Jacksonville to St. Augustine in 1885. Slowly moving south, the line reached Homestead in 1904. A year later, construction began to extend the railroad to Key West. With Cuba less than one hundred miles from Key West, Flagler envisioned his railroad as a conduit to greater trade with the Caribbean island.

It is little wonder that during construction the railroad was derisively called "Flagler's Folly." Conditions along the route were horrible; less hospitable land for construction could hardly be found. The heat of the Florida sun was nearly unbearable; mosquitoes, flies, alligators, and poisonous snakes all added to the burden. Blacks from Florida and the Bahamas were used for much of the backbreaking work of clearing dense underbrush. Recruited from southern and northern cities, skilled laborers were expected to repay their $12 one-way fare to the Keys. Workers received slightly more than a dollar a day for labor under very harsh conditions. By the time the railroad had been completed, several hundred men had died; construction costs approximated $25 million.

What had cost millions of dollars, great loss of life, and several years to complete was quickly destroyed on September 2, 1935. A Labor Day hurricane hit the Middle Keys with a vengeance, damaging much of the line and eroding tons of fill that had been used to lay the railroad bed. Even before the disaster, the railroad had been operating under financial difficulty. Now, although the damage was not beyond repair, the decision was made not to reconstruct the railroad. In one day, a project that had alternately been called "Flagler's Folly" and "The Eighth Wonder of the World" had ended. From the remains, however, a new project would arise as the railroad right-of-way was used for the roadbed of the new Overseas Highway that opened in 1938.

The hurricane of 1935 and the demise of the railroad were just two of the problems that Key West experienced in the 1930s. Key West had become one of America's poorest cities. The Great Depression had devastated the tiny island; individual fortunes had suffered a mighty reversal. By 1934, over three-quarters of the 11,000 local residents were receiving some kind of governmental financial assistance. Officially, Key West was in equally bad shape, having defaulted on its bond payments. In July 1934, the governor put the city government under the control of the Federal Emergency Relief Administration.

A revolution was about to begin. To reverse the dire financial straits, several far-reaching actions were taken. The coral-rock island was to undergo a metamorphosis into a tourist mecca. The controversial Julius Stone was assigned the job of turning Key West into a destination for vacationers with money to spend. Works Progress Administration artists were brought to Key West. Soon, government-sponsored works of art, large murals, and other cultural projects were appearing all over the city. Thousands of people assisted with the beautification of streets, houses, and landscapes. The Federal Building on Simonton Street was erected. With WPA funding, a bold new project, the world's first open-air aquarium, began to take shape at the foot of Whitehead Street in 1934. Initially, the community's first tourist attraction was owned by the city government and called the City Aquarium. Today, the Key West Aquarium is still a tourist attraction, but is privately owned.

The rejuvenation plan succeeded; Key West had a new industry—tourism. By the end of the winter of 1934–35, thousands of tourists had visited Key West for the first time. The numbers would continue to increase each year; many visitors would return again and again. Some would decide to stay permanently. While most were ordinary individuals looking for an out-of-the-ordinary vacation spot, some of those visitors were nationally known. President Harry Truman decided that the island was a perfect get-away spot, spending so much time there that his quarters at the Navy base became known as Truman's Little White House. Seemingly, Presidents Dwight D. Eisenhower and John F. Kennedy agreed, since they too vacationed there.

Quickly earning a reputation as an artistic haven, Key West has been home at one time or another to many prize-winning authors including Tennessee Williams, James Lee Herlihy, John Hersey, Wallace Stevens, Robert Frost, Phil Caputo, and Elizabeth Bishop. Ernest Hemmingway wrote five of his best-known works while he lived in the community. John James Audubon had visited Key West in 1832 to portray the flora and fauna of the islands. More than a century later, Hollywood moviemakers came to the Keys to create such popular films as *The Rose Tattoo*, *To Have and Have Not*, and more recently, *Speed II* and *True Lies*. Models can be seen posing on the beaches for sportswear catalog advertisements and the swimsuit edition of *Sports Illustrated*. Over the years, other celebrities such as Richard Burton, Elizabeth Taylor, Calvin Klein, Sally Rand, and Jimmy Buffett have enjoyed spending time in Key West.

Unlike many of the previous industries that came and went, the tourism industry has continued to grow and flourish. The tropical climate lures winter-weary visitors wishing to swim in crystal-clear water, snorkel on coral reefs, or just relax in the sunshine. Sportsmen pursue record-setting catches. For those with an interest in history, beautifully restored homes, guesthouses, museums, and commercial buildings fill the downtown historic area. Art galleries and eclectic shops line the streets, inciting purchases of everything from T-shirts to significant works of art. Restaurants provide a wide range of menus, from fresh seafood to a taste of the Caribbean, as well as the ever-popular key lime pie.

Key West is more than just a typical vacation spot, however. There is something special about the island. Dress codes are non-existent. The atmosphere is relaxed. The rules are different. Whether wishing to feed one's creativity, search for an illusory Margaritaville, or share in the free-spirited ambiance of "The Last Resort," opportunity abounds. Compete in a look-alike contest during Hemingway Days. Indulge your wildest dreams during Fantasy Fest. Relive the 1982 secession of Key West from the United States during the Conch Republic Independence Celebration. There's no need to wait for a special event, however. Hundreds gather at Mallory Square to celebrate the sunset every evening. Even more than any of its individual components, the state-of-mind that is the essence of Key West draws thousands of visitors annually to the "Southernmost City."

One

THEN AND NOW

Key West is an island just 4 miles long by 2 miles wide. Located at the very end of U.S. 1, the southernmost city in the continental United States is connected to the Florida mainland by the Overseas Highway. Counting those born in the Keys and generally known as "Conchs," as well as the newer residents, the city has just over 25,000 inhabitants. That number, however, fails to take into account the thousands of visitors who arrive on the island each year by boat, plane, and automobile. Some will visit the historical sites and study the local architecture, while others will be more interested in modern amenities. Many will spend their days sunning themselves on the beaches, diving on the coral reefs, or sailing on the brilliant blue water surrounding the Keys. Others will enjoy the nightlife of Duval Street. Some are looking for sunshine and warm weather and the chance to leave winter behind, while others are searching for something more elusive. Cultural pursuits, sports activities, artistic ambiance, or dreams of Margaritaville—all can be found in Key West. (Authors' Collection.)

Since 1885, trolleys have provided a way to get around Key West. Operated by the Key West Street Car Association, this horse-drawn conveyance came equipped with curtains that could be closed to shield passengers from inclement weather. The saloon the trolley is stopped in front of advertised a free lunch as an inducement to patrons. (Key West Art and Historical Society.)

The annual meeting of the Florida Press Association took place in Key West in March 1907. Attendees enjoyed a tour of the island aboard the electric railway cars operated by the Key West Electric Company. Known as "the playground of the people," La Brisa, with its dance pavilion, concerts, games, and amusements, was a favorite stop on the tour. (Monroe County Public Library.)

Although drinking establishments along the route no longer provide free lunches, today's visitors can still experience a trolley ride. Tour guides provide a running commentary on points of interest around the island for passengers aboard the Old Town Trolley. (Authors' Collection.)

The Key West Extension of the Florida East Coast Railway ceased operation after the line was partially destroyed in a hurricane in 1935. Today, the Conch Tour Train is the closest approximation of a railroad in Key West. More than ten million visitors have filled the passenger cars of the propane-fueled motorized tram on sightseeing tours of the island. (Authors' Collection.)

Long before ice began to be manufactured in Key West in 1890, ships transported natural ice from New England. During the mid-1800s, entrepreneur Asa F. Tift built an icehouse adjacent to the ship chandlery and cisterns previously constructed as part of A.C. Tift and Company. The oldest commercial buildings in Key West, the former chandlery currently houses the chamber of commerce. Framed by its distinctive double doors, the icehouse is now home to the Shell Warehouse. (Monroe County Public Library and Authors' Collection.)

Erected in 1879, this Wall & Company warehouse was one of the earliest brick structures in Key West. William H. Wall, considered to be one of the community's pioneers, arrived on the island after being shipwrecked. As did many Key Westers of the era, Wall made his fortune in salvaged goods. In 1881, the nearly 154-foot-long building was sold to Asa F. Tift to become part of his waterfront chandlery. Although damage from the 1886 fire necessitated a new roof and some masonry repair, the building remains much as it was in 1879. Today, the warehouse is the site of Cayo Hueso y Habana, a restaurant and retail shop commemorating the contributions of people of Spanish/Cuban heritage. A reproduction of the aircraft used by Augustin Parla in his 1913 flight from Key West to Cuba hangs inside. (Monroe County Public Library and Authors' Collection.)

The Oldest House, Key West, Florida — Built in 1825 Entirely of Cedar

This one-story house built of cedar in the 1820s is believed to be the oldest house in Key West. Constructed by a ship's carpenter, it was originally located on the corner of Caroline and Whitehead Streets. Around 1832, by means of mule teams and lots of muscle, the house was moved to its present location at 322 Duval Street. In 1839, Capt. Frances Watlington purchased the residence. Donated to the State of Florida in 1974, the house is operated today as the Wrecker's Museum, and serves as a reminder of the role that the wrecking industry played in making Key West what it is today. (Authors' Collection.)

This small wood-framed building on the southwest end of Mallory Square was constructed around 1889. Used first as the ticket office for the Southern Express Company and later for Mallory Steamship Lines, it was originally built on lot 4, square 3, of a piece of property known in the 1890s as Tift's Wharf. During the transformation of the dock area in the 1960s into the landscaped public space of today, the structure was moved to its present location to serve as Hospitality House. It is the headquarters of the Old Island Restoration Foundation, one of Key West's historic preservation organizations. (Monroe County Public Library and Authors' Collection.)

The Custom House was designed by William Kerr, an Irishman from Ballybole, County Down. Since local building supplies were unavailable for the construction of a facility of this magnitude, materials and labor were imported. Nearly 1 million bricks were fired and transported from New York; iron was smelted and shipped from Pennsylvania. Masons were brought from Massachusetts, while other skilled craftsmen were recruited from all over the United States. (Key West Art and Historical Society.)

A Civil War monument stands in a small triangular park just in front of the Custom House and the former Naval Coal Depot, Building 1. Erected by the Navy Club of Key West in 1866, it is dedicated "to the memory of the officers, sailors, and soldiers of the Army, Navy, and Marine Corps of the United States who lost their lives in the country's service upon this station from 1861 to 1865." A small wrought-iron fence contributed by Jeptha V. Harris, a Confederate veteran, encircles the monument. (Key West Art and Historical Society.)

Built at a cost of nearly $108,000 to house the federal offices of the courts, customs, postal, and lighthouse services, the U.S. Custom House came to life in 1891 after three years of construction. Located next to the teeming wharf area filled with chandleries, warehouses, piers, and ships from around the world, the facility handled the myriad aspects of maritime commerce. (Key West Art and Historical Society.)

When a new federal building provided quarters for all of the federal agencies except the U.S. Lighthouse Service, the Custom House became the Naval Administration Building. As more offices were needed over the years, the building suffered a number of inappropriate additions and destructive alterations. As this photograph shows, the beauty of the original building became harder and harder to see. (Monroe County Public Library.)

Custom House,
Key West, Fla.

An example of late-19th-century eclectic architecture complete with Queen Anne and Richardsonian Romanesque features, the Custom House had been a magnificent and unique structure originally. An extensive $9 million, ten-year restoration effort has returned the structure to its former elegance. In 1999, the building opened as the Key West Museum of Art and History at the Custom House. More than 100 years after its original construction, visitors can once again see the finely crafted architectural details of the building while enjoying a variety of exhibits dealing with the art and history of Key West. (Key West Art and Historical Society and Authors' Collection.)

United States Weather Bureau, Key West, Florida

Complete with telegraph antenna and outdoor weather forecasting equipment, this masonry structure was erected in 1911 to house the United States Weather Bureau in Key West. Located at the southernmost point in the continental United States, the weather station was in the best position to provide early warning of impending tropical storms. Currently the building welcomes guests as the Weatherstation Inn. It is one of 23 buildings that comprise a National Register of Historic Places District on the grounds of the old naval station, now part of the upscale gated community of Truman Annex. (Authors' Collection.)

Built as an aid to maritime navigation in 1825, the original Key West lighthouse was located on the tip of the island. When a hurricane in 1846 destroyed the structure, the decision was made to construct its replacement further from the shoreline. Stephen Mallory, the Key West customs collector, purchased the property from John Whitehead for the sum of $200. The U.S. Lighthouse Service operated the station. (Key West Art and Historical Society.)

Turned over to the Coast Guard in 1939, the lighthouse was originally manned around the clock. Located next door to the lighthouse, the lighthouse keeper's quarters provided on-the-job housing for the keeper and his assistants until the light was electrified in 1917. On three separate occasions during the operational history of the Key West lighthouse, the job of keeper was held by a woman. (Key West Art and Historical Society.)

Postcards touted the landmark's claim to fame as the only lighthouse in America entirely within the city limits. Built further inland at 938 Whitehead Street after the hurricane of 1846, the third oldest brick lighthouse in Florida was 56 feet high, on a site an additional 14 feet above sea level. When the multi-storied buildings resulting from Key West's growth obscured the lighthouse's beacon, 20 feet were added to the structure in the 1890s. (Key West Art and Historical Society.)

The sight of the Key West lighthouse still evokes long-gone images of three-masted sailing ships entering the island's harbor. Even while the lighthouse was in active operation, it was still a tourist destination. An 1882 edition of *Florida for Tourists, Invalids, and Settlers* touted it as an interesting place to visit. The lighthouse and the lighthouse keeper's quarters were decommissioned in 1969. In 1972, the Key West Art and Historical Society reopened the site as the Key West Lighthouse Museum. (Edward Swanick.)

Visitors today can climb the 88-step spiral staircase to the top of the lighthouse and treat themselves to a breathtaking panoramic view of the city. Two photographs, one taken during the 1940s and a similar image taken in 2000, show a remarkable similarity with many of the buildings shown in the earlier image still in existence. Unlike many communities that suffered the wholesale destruction that frequently accompanied urban renewal, Key West has been fortunate to retain many of the historic structures that make it unique. (Key West Art and Historical Society and Authors' Collection.)

Unless it is very early in the day, visitors will seldom see Duval Street as unoccupied as it is in either of these photographs taken some 80 years apart. Extending from the Gulf of Mexico to the Atlantic Ocean and named in honor of William P. Duval, the first territorial governor of Florida, it is perhaps Key West's best-known thoroughfare. Lined with guest accommodations, restaurants, bars, art galleries, and gift shops, Duval Street is normally the scene of a constant parade of tourists. Whether a T-shirt or a work of art, a cold beer or a gourmet meal, a temporary tattoo or a piece of designer jewelry, Duval Street has something for everyone. It is, however, only part of the story of Key West. (Monroe County Public Library and Authors' Collection.)

The Key West Aquarium, built by Depression-era workers from the Federal Emergency Relief Administration, is considered to be Key West's original tourist attraction. Billed as the world's first open-air aquarium, an idea suggested by the director of Philadelphia's Fairmount Park Aquarium, the city-owned facility at the foot of Whitehead Street opened after two years of construction. (Authors' Collection.)

Still in its original location, today the Key West Aquarium is privately owned. While the building's Whitehead Street facade looks virtually unchanged, the facility is no longer completely open to the Florida sunshine. An extensive renovation in the 1980s enclosed the open-air aquarium, permitting visitors to enjoy the displays of marine life indigenous to the Florida Keys regardless of the weather. (Authors' Collection.)

In this promotional photograph from the 1960s, tourists enjoyed feeding sea turtles housed in open tanks at the aquarium. Today, the Key West Aquarium participates in the Green Sea Turtle Head Start program, providing a secure environment for baby turtles' first year of life and increasing their chances of survival in the wild. (Monroe County Public Library.)

Indoor touch tanks provide interactive encounters with marine life, while daily shark, stingray, and sawfish feedings are part of the entertainment. Visitors also have the opportunity to view tarpon, snook, jacks, and other Florida fish from a wooden boardwalk encircling the outdoor Atlantic Shores exhibit. (Authors' Collection.)

On the day this photograph was taken, the Strand Theater advertised two feature films—*The Westerner*, starring Gary Cooper, and *The Walls of Jericho* with Kirk Douglas. Possibly even more of an inducement than the movies themselves, however, were the signs advertising "air conditioned for your comfort" and inviting patrons to "enjoy two full hours of top entertainment here in comfort." (Monroe County Public Library.)

Today, the Strand Theater, located at 527 Duval Street, no longer shows the most popular films of the day. The ornate structure is instead home to Ripley's Believe It or Not! Odditorium. In lieu of Hollywood stars engaged in cinematic adventures, collections of exotica ranging from shrunken heads to gigantic hammerhead sharks provide entertainment. (Authors' Collection.)

Two
PEOPLE, PLACES, AND EVENTS

In the 1820s, the seas surrounding Key West were very dangerous; pirates roamed at will, plundering merchant ships in the Caribbean and along the trade routes through the Gulf of Mexico. In 1822, Capt. David Porter of the U.S. Navy was appointed commodore of the West Indies anti-pirate squadron, based at Key West. Porter arrived in Key West in April 1823, with orders to protect American citizens from pirates, suppress the slave trade, and establish a naval base at Key West. All this he accomplished with a mosquito fleet consisting of eight shallow-draft schooners, five 20-oared barges, and the USS *Seagull*, supposedly the first steam-powered warship to be used in active service. Porter used the old post office as his quarters. When he left Key West in 1825, the building became the original customs house in a city that was rapidly changing. From a total population of barely 400 people in 1823, Key West grew to more than 500 inhabitants in 1830. Twenty years later, more than 2,500 called the city home. (Key West Art and Historical Society.)

John W. Simonton might be considered the father of Key West. For the sum of $2,000, he purchased the island from Juan Pablo Salas in December 1821, and then proceeded to sell off three portions. While he dabbled at several occupations in Key West, including merchant and salt manufacturer, much of his time was actually spent in Mobile and Washington, D.C. Simonton Street is named in his honor. (Monroe County Public Library.)

A stroll along Whitehead Street begins at the aquarium and ends at the southernmost point in the continental United States. Whitehead Street is named for John Whitehead, one of Key West's founders who had purchased a major portion of Key West from John Simonton. Whitehead served as a merchant, a banker, and in the insurance business, before leaving Key West for New Orleans in 1832. (Monroe County Public Library.)

Stephen R. Mallory studied law under the tutelage of William Marvin and served as a county judge and as the customs collector. Elected to the Senate in 1851, he served as the secretary of the navy for the Confederacy. Imprisoned for ten months after the Civil War, Mallory later lived in Pensacola until his death in 1873. The name given to Mallory Square recognizes both his contributions and the former site of the Clyde Mallory Steamship Company docks. (Key West Art and Historical Society.)

The Jefferson Hotel on Duval Street offered a perfect panoramic view of Key West with the harbor in the background. In the foreground are several wooden cigar factories along Ann Street. These factories, along with most of the downtown business district, would subsequently be destroyed in the catastrophic fire of 1886. (Monroe County Public Library.)

Local citizens have chosen a unique way to recognize the contributions of a number of early residents. The Key West Historic Memorial Sculpture Garden sits along the original shoreline in Mallory Square. Thirty-six bronze busts depict the men and women "who made Key West such a vibrant and important outpost of American culture and folklore." (Authors' Collection.)

Created by James Mastin, an intricately detailed sculpture is the centerpiece of the Sculpture Garden. Entitled "The Wreckers," it depicts the local residents who made their living by coming to the aid of vessels in distress. Before lighthouses reduced the incidence of shipwrecks on the reefs surrounding the Keys and the Coast Guard took over the role of lifesaving, wreckers rescued first the crews and passengers and then the cargoes of ships aground. (Authors' Collection.)

One of the busts in the Key West Historic Memorial Sculpture Garden depicts Sandy Cornish, a leader of the local African-American community. Born a slave in Maryland around 1793, "Uncle Sandy" was brought to Florida in 1839. He succeeded in buying his freedom, only to be recaptured by slave traders several years later. Escaping his captors, Cornish came to Key West in the late 1840s. He and his wife, Lillah, supplied the town with fruits and vegetables grown on their farm near what is today Truman Avenue and Simonton Street. (Authors' Collection.)

One of the wealthiest men in Key West, Sandy Cornish established the Cornish Chapel of the African Methodist Episcopal Church on Whitehead Street in 1864. African Americans have played important roles in both the economic and cultural life of Key West since its beginning. Just a small part of the city's early population, African Americans in 1890 comprised nearly one-third of Key West's inhabitants. (Monroe County Public Library.)

Founded in 1871 by Cuban exiles to promote and preserve Cuban cultural values, the Instituto Patriotic y Docente San Carlos was first located on Ann Street. A move to a new larger facility in 1874 proved only temporary when the building was the origin of the 1886 fire. Until its destruction in the 1919 hurricane, its replacement featured a school on the upper floor and an opera house that doubled as a meeting place for the Cuban community on the ground level. (Monroe County Public Library.)

Constructed in 1924 on Duval Street, the present San Carlos Institute is a center for Cuban history and heritage. A recent $4 million restoration returned the building, deteriorated to the point of being slated for demolition in 1985, to its former glory. Designed by Francisco Centurion, a prominent Cuban architect, and incorporating many elements of Cuban architecture, the San Carlos Institute today serves as a library, art gallery, museum, school, theater, and conference center. (Monroe County Public Library.)

San Carlos Institute is named after Cuba's Seminario San Carlos and in honor of Carlos Manuel de Cespedes, father of the ten-year Cuban fight for independence. In 1868, it was de Cespedes who sounded the cry, "Cuba Libre." Among the works of art that decorate the lobby of San Carlos Institute is this painting by Joe Regan. The subject is, of course, Carlos Manuel de Cespedes. (Authors' Collection.)

Jose Marti, Cuban poet and patriot, also has a prominent place in the history of San Carlos Institute. Terming the center "La Casa Cuba," Marti addressed members of the Cuban community in Key West as he launched his drive for Cuban independence in 1892. One hundred years later, on January 3, 1992, 5,000 people attended the reopening ceremonies of the San Carlos Institute. (Monroe County Public Library.)

One of the most significant events that shaped Key West was the catastrophic fire of 1886. The fire was of gigantic proportions, consuming nearly 50 acres. Everything in its path—homes, municipal buildings, stores, and cigar factories—was destroyed. Describing the destruction, the Jacksonville, Florida, *Times-Union* newspaper said, "The ruins present a most mournful appearance, reminding one of a great cemetery." (Monroe County Public Library.)

A watchman at the San Carlos discovered the fire at approximately 1:45 a.m. on March 30, 1886. Fanned by the wind, the flames raced through the business district toward the wharves. The 12-hour fire had consumed an area one mile long and one-third of a mile wide. The city's largest industry, the cigar factories, no longer existed. More than 4,000 people were unemployed. Thousands were homeless. Property losses were estimated at nearly $2 million, most of which was uninsured. (Monroe County Public Library.)

Under the direction of Fire Chief Benjamin Franklin H. Bowers, the city's three volunteer companies valiantly battled the conflagration. Military personnel in Key West assisted in fighting the fire, but to no avail. In a city consisting almost entirely of wooden structures, the fire department's equipment was outdated and insufficient. An adequate water supply didn't exist; there were no wells and during the dry season, cisterns contained little water. (Alex Vega.)

After the fire, positive changes—construction of several new fire stations, increases in manpower, and the acquisition of new firefighting equipment—resulted. Citizens were determined not to repeat a situation newspapers described as "crowds of wretched humanity, disheveled and haggard, smoke begrimed and scorched, exhausted with fatigue and heat, some half crazed, and not a few with bandages. Ruin broods over the town and within a week starvation will stalk through the streets which are not already in ashes." (Florida State Archives.)

Nature also had a role in shaping Key West. Located in the semi-tropics and surrounded by the waters of the Atlantic Ocean and the Gulf of Mexico, the Keys were frequently buffeted by the high winds, raging seas, and heavy rains that accompany tropical storms and hurricanes. As early as 1622, several treasure-laden Spanish ships sank in a storm just west of the Dry Tortugas. Devastating hurricanes also hit the Keys in 1846, 1876, 1909, 1910, 1919, 1935, and 1960. (Key West Art and Historical Society.)

Warnings of hurricanes today come far in advance of the actual storms, thanks to modern weather forecasting technology and advances in communication. In the not-too-distant past, however, this wasn't the case. Residents of the Keys would frequently awaken to find the fury of a tropical storm—or even worse, a full-fledged hurricane—on their doorsteps, literally and figuratively. Homes, churches, and cigar factories all proved vulnerable to the storms' fury. (Key West Art and Historical Society.)

On October 11, 1909, one of the most intense hurricanes ever recorded to that date in Florida hit the Keys. Winds were clocked at 94 miles per hour, accompanied by 8 to 10 inches of rain. At Sand Key, the weather bureau building was swept out to sea. In Key West, more than 400 buildings were washed away by the tide or collapsed by the high winds. Wooden houses surrounding the cigar factories were turned into kindling. (Key West Art and Historical Society.)

Fifteen people were reported killed in the storm. Telegraph poles toppled in the wind. Key West was filled with debris as entire buildings floated off their foundations and into the streets. In the harbor, more than 300 boats were destroyed. Portions of the Florida East Coast Overseas Railroad, still under construction, were washed away. (Key West Art and Historical Society.)

La Brisa, a favorite recreational spot in Key West, suffered major damage. Porches collapsed; high winds removed the dome from the roof of the local landmark and deposited it alongside the building. The city reported over $1 million in damage from the hurricane. A year later, another storm would carry away many of the structures that had managed to escape destruction in 1909. (Key West Art and Historical Society.)

While the Labor Day hurricane of September 2, 1935, did only minimal damage in Key West, it had devastating consequences further north. The Hurricane Monument on Upper Matecumbe Key serves as a memorial to the hundreds of victims lost in the disaster. Carved from local rock by WPA artists, the monument was dedicated in 1937 and added to the National Register of Historic Places in 1995. (Authors' Collection.)

Twenty-three years after Henry Flagler's dream of a railroad to Key West had become reality, a Labor Day hurricane would turn that dream into a nightmare and spell the end of the rail line. Wind gusts of 150 to 200 miles per hour and 18- to 20-foot tides at Islamorada swept away buildings, 35 miles of railroad track, and even most of the rescue train sent to evacuate residents and some 300 World War I veterans who were building the new Overseas Highway. Only a handful of people survived. (Key West Art and Historical Society.)

Until the disastrous hurricane of 1935, the Overseas Railroad brought thousands of people to Key West each year. From Miami, the train traveled down the Keys, ending at the docks where passengers could then board steamers to carry them to Cuba, just 90 miles away. During Prohibition, returning baggage labeled "clothing" but filled with gurgling liquids was a common phenomenon. (Key West Art and Historical Society.)

A native New Yorker born in 1830, Henry M. Flagler would have a profound and long-lasting influence on Florida and especially the island of Key West. Along with John D. Rockefeller, he started the Standard Oil Company in 1870, amassing a personal fortune in the process. In 1885, Flagler purchased a short line railroad operating between Jacksonville and St. Augustine, and began extending it south to Miami. By 1904, the railroad had reached Homestead. A visionary, Flagler saw the potential of the Panama Canal, as well as increased trade with Cuba. Arguing that Key West would be the perfect intermediary point to take advantage of both, he proposed the extension of his railroad down the chain of islands to Key West. Few people supported the idea; detractors derided the idea as "Flagler's Folly." Nevertheless, Flagler remained steadfast and in 1905 began construction. (Key West Art and Historical Society.)

Flagler's dream of a "railroad that goes to sea" required much more than his multi-million-dollar investment. It took manpower—and lots of it. Flagler's workers literally created something from nothing as they built roadbeds, bridges, and viaducts through water, sand, and swamp. Construction camps housing laborers who faced the threats of hurricanes, alligators, and rattlesnakes dotted the Keys. (Key West Art and Historical Society.)

The job of building Flagler's railroad in the middle of water obviously required a fleet of ships. The armada included launches, houseboats, steamers, and workboats complete with cranes and pile drivers. Everything, including workers, supplies, and materials, had to be ferried to the jobsite. Ocean-going vessels transported raw materials from Florida's mainland. Thousands of laborers worked day and night to build a 128-mile stretch of railroad track in the midst of nothing. (Key West Art and Historical Society.)

As roadbeds grew from the sea and tracks were laid, the job became slightly easier. Workers and equipment could now be brought to the construction site over the completed tracks. Land-based work camps were erected on filled sites that had previously been under water. There were dormitories, offices, medical dispensaries, stores, churches, and recreational facilities. There was, however, no alcohol. Flagler, a strict teetotaler, banned liquor in his work camps. (Key West Art and Historical Society.)

The tracks over the sea that seemingly went nowhere covered 128 miles from Homestead to Key West. At the end of the journey lay Key West and more specifically, Trumbo Point. As Flagler's workmen had done so many times before, they again created something from nothing—Trumbo Point. Named in honor of project engineer Howard Trumbo, a 134-acre railroad yard was created from dredged fill. The small island of Key West had finally been linked to Florida's mainland. (Key West Art and Historical Society.)

On January 22, 1912, seven years after construction had begun, the Florida East Coast railroad's *Extension Special*, pulling Flagler's private coach, arrived in Key West. The cost of constructing what many described as "The Eighth Wonder of the World" had been high—an estimated $25 million and several hundred lives. Nonetheless, it was a feat many had predicted could not be accomplished. (Key West Art and Historical Society.)

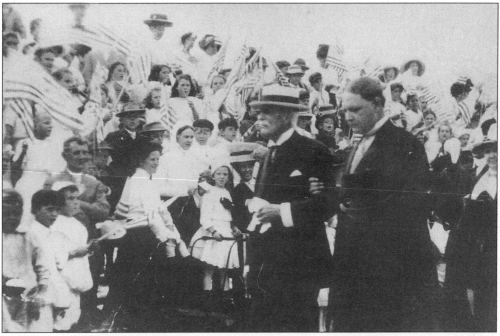

The completion of the Key West Extension of the Florida East Coast Railway was heralded by a grand celebration. Bands, parades, and throngs of admiring Key West residents of all ages turned out to welcome the elderly Henry Flagler. His dream of a passenger railroad connecting Key West to the mainland had been realized. Unfortunately, Flagler died the following year, having been able to enjoy his accomplishment for only a short time. (Key West Art and Historical Society.)

Just a few years after America's entrance into the world of aviation, Key West entered the record books as the starting point of the world's record over-water flight—a monumental 89.78 miles. John A.D. McCurdy set out on the morning of January 30, 1911, to fly across the Straits of Florida to Havana, Cuba. Although a broken oil line caused his aircraft to land in the water just ten miles short of his goal, McCurdy was awarded an $8,000 prize for his accomplishment. (Monroe County Public Library.)

Augustin Parla fought to the bitter end to be the first man to fly the Straits of Florida from Key West to Cuba and claim the $10,000 prize offered by the City of Havana. Born in Key West in 1887, Parla learned to fly at the Curtiss flying school in Miami in 1912. His date with destiny arrived on May 17, 1913, when he attempted the flight in his recently purchased Curtiss airplane. (Monroe County Public Library.)

Unfortunately for Parla, Domingo Rosillo also wanted the fame and fortune associated with such a flight. Both took off on May 17, but damage to Parla's aircraft caused his flight to be aborted. Rosillo successfully made the flight, won the prize, and set a new record for distance flying. Two days later, on May 19, 1913, Parla made a record-setting flight of 117.5 miles, eclipsing Rosillo's accomplishment. The Cuban government awarded him a $5,000 prize for his effort. (Key West Art and Historical Society.)

Aeromarine Airways inaugurated regular scheduled air service between Key West and Havana, Cuba, on November 1, 1920. From a waterfront lot between Duval and Simonton Streets, the airline carried both passengers and mail on the 90-mile trip. In 1921, Aeromarine began its "High-Ball Express," using converted Navy F5-L planes on the two-day flight between New York and Havana, with stops in Atlantic City, Beaufort, Miami, and Key West. Aeromarine ceased operations in 1924. (Key West Art and Historical Society.)

A new airline, Pan American Airways, received a mail contract on July 19, 1927, authorizing operation between Key West, Florida, and Havana, Cuba. To meet the contract deadline for beginning service, Pan Am chartered a Fairchild FC-2 float plane named *La Niña* from West Indian Aerial Express to fly from Key West to Havana on October 19. (Monroe County Public Library.)

Following receipt of the mail contract, Pan American ordered three Fokker F-VII trimotors, but hadn't taken delivery yet. Construction of the company-commissioned runway at Key West's Meacham Field was not finished. Finally, on October 28, 1927, the new fully equipped airline started its regularly scheduled mail runs from Key West to Havana. (Florida State Archives.)

Although Pan American's passenger service from Key West to Havana did not begin until January 16, 1928, the service was immediately popular. For a one-way fare of $50, more than 1,100 tickets were sold the first year. While the southbound flight took only 75 minutes, wind currents added an extra 15 minutes to the return flight. This building served as Pan Am's first Key West office. Kelly's, a popular restaurant filled with aviation memorabilia located on the corner of Caroline and Whitehead Streets, occupies the structure more than 70 years later. (Authors' Collection.)

Robert E. Hamilton died in June 1943 at the age of 110 years and 11 months. A resident of Key West for a dozen years, he came from the Ten Thousand Islands and could frequently be seen tending his boat along the shore of Garrison Bight. At the age of 104, he applied for a job with the WPA in Key West, aggressively asserting his agility and ability to work despite his advanced years. Noteworthy for more than his longevity, Hamilton could be said to typify the changes that had occurred in the Southernmost City. According to his obituary, he had been a slave, a soldier, and a sailor. Key West had also seen drastic changes over the years. Newcomers of various ethnic backgrounds had arrived; different ways of earning a living had succeeded and failed. The city had experienced both war and peacetime, wealth and poverty. (Key West Art and Historical Society.)

Three

A Military Presence

Rising like an apparition from the sea, Fort Zachary Taylor was built on an almost 13-acre island located near Whitehead Spit on the southwest shore of Key West. Originally set in 10 feet of water approximately 440 yards offshore, the fort was connected to the mainland by a 720-foot-long wooden causeway, complete with a drawbridge. Construction of the fort, originally designed as part of Florida's coastal defense system, began in November 1845, and was finally completed at the end of the Civil War. Progress was frequently impeded by outbreaks of yellow fever that proved fatal to many of the workers. Less than a year after construction started, the hurricane of October 11, 1846, left a path of destruction. Four workers drowned in the storm, while much of their work was also eradicated. Built of brick and local coral rock and named after President Zachary Taylor, who died in 1850, the fort was finally completed in 1866. (Monroe County Public Library.)

In 1861, at the beginning of the Civil War, Union troops led by Capt. James Brannan took over Fort Taylor, preventing its control by local Confederate sympathizers. As a result of his actions, Key West remained in Union control throughout the war. No longer an active military installation, today Fort Zachary Taylor is operated by the National Park Service as a historical site. (Key West Art and Historical Society.)

Maj. James Glassel of the U.S. Army and two companies of infantry arrived in Key West in February 1831. They set up camp on the northern side of the island near the present site of White Street and Palm Avenue. Glassel's troops erected officers' quarters, barracks, a guard house, and several smaller buildings. This encampment became known as the Key West Barracks, and as pictured here in 1891, had grown in both size and sophistication. (Key West Art and Historical Society.)

At the beginning of the Civil War, two onshore fortifications were begun to provide additional protection for Fort Taylor. Before work could be completed on either the East or West Martello towers, however, construction was suspended. Formerly considered impenetrable, advances in weaponry had made such masonry structures obsolete. (Authors' Collection.)

The East and West Martello towers have both been placed on the National Register of Historic Places. Today, the Key West Art and Historical Society operates the East Martello tower as the East Martello Museum. Historical exhibits, as well as works of art by Stanley Papio and Mario Sanchez, are displayed within the 8-foot-thick brick walls of the fortification. The West Martello tower is a tropical haven of exotic flora maintained by the Key West Garden Club. (Key West Art and Historical Society.)

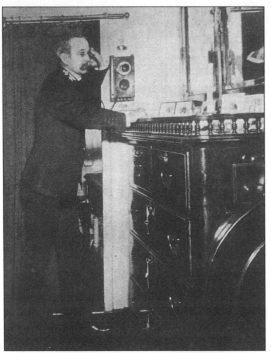

Capt. Charles D. Sigsbee served as commander of the USS *Maine*. On the night of February 15, 1898, the ship exploded as it lay at anchor in Havana Harbor, sending 266 Americans to their deaths. Of the destruction of the *Maine*, Sigsbee recalled, "She had settled in the mud and her poop-deck, where we had stood at the last possible moment, was under water." (Key West Art and Historical Society.)

A group of petty officers assigned to the USS *Maine* posed for posterity. Little did they know that an explosion of undetermined origin would soon sink their ship, causing great loss of life. Of the 24 men pictured here, 11 died in the disaster. Reviewing the carnage, Captain Sigsbee wrote, "On the white part of the ceiling was the impression of two human bodies—mere dust— so I was told afterward." (Key West Art and Historical Society.)

Warships such as the USS *Maine* came to symbolize America's growing military strength as the 19th century drew to a close. The *Maine* arrived in Key West on December 15, 1897. On January 24, 1898, Captain Sigsbee received orders to proceed to Havana Harbor to protect American citizens in Cuba. Twenty-two days later on February 15, the unthinkable happened—the USS *Maine* exploded. (Key West Art and Historical Society.)

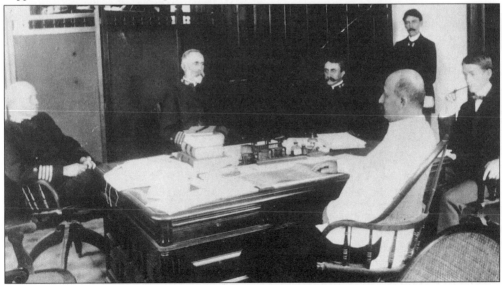

Following the sinking of the USS *Maine* in the harbor of Havana, Cuba, a Naval Court of Inquiry was convened in the second-floor courtroom at the Custom House in Key West to investigate the destruction of the American warship. Captain Sigsbee was exonerated of any blame for the incident. (Key West Art and Historical Society.)

Maine Monument, Erected in Honor of the Sailors Sunk in Havana Harbor, Key West, Florida

"Remember the *Maine*" was an oft-heard slogan near the end of the 19th century. The phrase, of course, referred to the sinking of the USS *Maine* in Havana Harbor, Cuba, on February 15, 1898, and the resulting loss of American lives. While allegations were never proven, Americans excited by sensational journalism and jingoism blamed Spain for the devastating destruction of an American battleship. Two months later, on April 21, 1898, with a declaration of war against Spain, the Spanish-American War had begun. A reminder of the tragedy can be seen at the Key West Cemetery. Located near the cemetery's Margaret Street entrance, a 105-foot-by-160-foot enclosure contains the *Maine* Monument. Surrounded by a cast-iron fence, the centerpiece is a full-sized sculpture of a sailor from the USS *Maine* standing atop a granite pedestal. More than one hundred years old, the monument was erected in 1898 through the joint efforts of the citizens of Key West and the Encampment Union Veteran Legion so that people would forever "Remember the *Maine*." (Authors' Collection.)

Key West still served as a naval installation during peacetime, albeit on a smaller scale. In February 1907, the USS *Hopkins*, a torpedo boat destroyer, put into Key West to have a broken port propeller repaired. The cause of the accident is unknown; perhaps the propeller was sheared off when the vessel came in contact with one of the coral reefs surrounding the Keys. (Key West Art and Historical Society.)

In 1908, band concerts and dress parades at Fort Zachary Taylor provided a pleasurable way for local residents to spend a Sunday afternoon. The 9th Artillery Band, pictured here in front of the barracks, also frequently entertained visiting dignitaries, both military and civilian. In addition to the typical musical instruments for military bands, the 9th Artillery Band's equipment included a harp. (Key West Art and Historical Society.)

Headquarters of the 7th Naval District, the command at Key West included the naval station, as well as a submarine base and a naval aviation training facility. A major part of the installation's responsibilities during World War I was the daily patrol in search of German submarine activity in the Atlantic Ocean and the Gulf of Mexico. (Key West Art and Historical Society.)

The United States entered World War I on April 6, 1917. Short of men, equipment, and bases, the Navy was woefully unprepared. Immediate action was necessary. Land at Trumbo Point was leased from the Florida East Coast Railway, and on July 13, 1917, ground was broken for the Key West Naval Air Station. After months of hurried construction, the Key West Naval Air Station was commissioned on December 18, 1917. (Key West Art and Historical Society.)

Part of the construction at the installation included this giant dirigible hangar. The following February, the station's dirigibles and observation balloons, in concert with Navy seaplanes operating from the Dry Tortugas, began daily anti-submarine patrols against feared German attacks. The Key West Naval Air Station was decommissioned in 1920, only to be reactivated at the onset of World War II. (Key West Art and Historical Society.)

In 1917, this U.S. Navy blimp was operating out of Key West. By 1918, the Key West Naval Air Station was functioning at near peak capacity. The seaplane training center and the blimp facility were fully established, while the base included three ramps, an administration building, barracks, a hangar for patrol blimps, and a hydrogen generator plant. (Key West Art and Historical Society.)

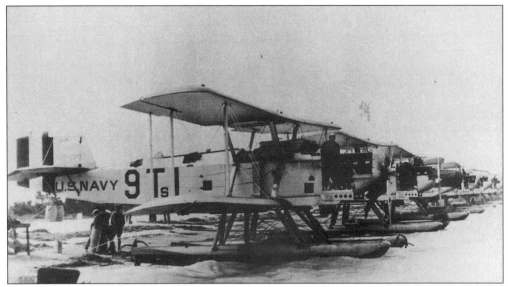

These Curtiss aircraft were part of the aerial fleet assigned to the Key West Naval Air Station at Trumbo Point in 1918. Commanded by the 7th Naval District, the airplanes and blimps at the air station, along with ocean-going vessels, patrolled the surrounding waters of the Gulf and Atlantic to protect against German submarines and keep them from obtaining Mexican oil. (Key West Art and Historical Society.)

While we tend to think of camouflaged buildings, vehicles, and clothing as a modern occurrence, this 1918 photograph of warehouses at the Key West Naval Station shows how incorrect that idea would be. Such techniques were obviously in use during World War I. The tall crane-like apparatus is a coaling rig used to load coal onto vessels that put into Key West for refueling. (Key West Art and Historical Society.)

A 10-inch rifled cannon nearly 15 feet long and weighing thousands of pounds is dragged through the streets of Key West during World War I for positioning at the Mahlon D. Ford battery at Fort Taylor. Although the cannon had originally been intended for use during the Spanish-American War, it didn't arrive in Key West until after the end of the hostilities. (Monroe County Public Library.)

Troops were assigned to Fort Taylor during both World War I and World War II. Although supporting batteries had been added earlier, a modern battery was built inside the fort after the upper two stories were removed in 1899. While the cannons at Fort Taylor were never actually fired against America's enemies, artillery practice was still a necessary part of a soldier's training. (Monroe County Public Library.)

Navy submarines such as this one in dry-dock at Key West played a role in patrolling the Atlantic Ocean and Gulf of Mexico during World War I. As evidenced by the torpedoing of the *Lusitania* on May 7, 1915, off the coast of Ireland, German U-boats were deadly. While American submarines undoubtedly acted as a deterrent to German subs near Florida, their role in World War I was relatively minor. (Key West Art and Historical Society.)

On March 19, 1917, the U.S. Navy authorized the enlistment of women. Officially designated a yeoman-f, a woman serving in the Navy commonly became known as a yeomanette, a lady sailor, or a yeowoman. By the end of World War I, 11,275 yeomenettes had served in the U.S. Navy as clerical workers, translators, and radio operators and in recruitment and bond drives. Several Key West women including Jennie DeBoer served their country as yeomenettes during World War I. (Key West Art and Historical Society.)

Members of the Naval Reserve dressed in their "whites" as they paraded down Key West's Duval Street in 1917. During World War I, the city was home to thousands of sailors from all over America. Many were assigned to duty at the naval station, naval air station, or submarine base; others were from visiting naval vessels that put into Key West for coal and supplies. (Key West Art and Historical Society.)

After years of conflict, the Great War, the "war to end all wars," was finally over. Fighting stopped at 11 a.m. on November 11, 1918. As the long-awaited news was heard in towns large and small across America, people rejoiced. Whistles blew, church bells rang, and children and adults ran through the streets in celebration. Uncle Sam led Key Westers in an Armistice Day parade on Duval Street. (Monroe County Public Library.)

The Key West Naval Station had played an important role in southern naval operations since its founding in 1822. From its inception, it was a key to the Caribbean, Gulf trade routes, and the countries of Central and South America. During World War II, more than 14,000 ships logged into Key West. The island quickly came to be considered "The Gibraltar of the Gulf." (Key West Art and Historical Society.)

Civilian and military personnel labored side-by-side on expansion of the base in March 1942. On a bare maintenance status since June 1932, the Key West Naval Station was reopened on November 1, 1939, as war raged in Europe. By the end of the war, the station had grown from 50 to 767 acres of land, excluding some 2,455 acres occupied by the naval air station. (Monroe County Public Library.)

Key West-based submarines were an important part of the war effort during World War II. Their primary mission was to provide services to the fleet training program. Secondary missions included assistance in development of new devices such as sono-buoys and the bathy-thermograph, as well as serving as a deterrent to German submarines and ships operating in the Atlantic and Gulf of Mexico. (Monroe County Public Library.)

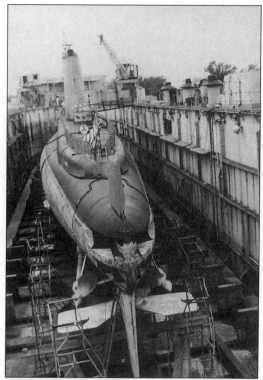

During World War II, Meacham Field, Key West's civilian airport, was used for military operations. Originally pressed into service as an Army Air Corps facility, by July 1943, command had been transferred to the Navy. Runways were expanded during 1943 to include four hard-surfaced runways of rolled marl. Four U.S. Navy blimps were also stationed at Meacham during World War II. (Key West Art and Historical Society.)

The Martello towers had a long tradition in the service of the U.S. military. Planned as part of a five-fort system to protect the land approaches to Fort Taylor, only the East and West Martello towers were ever built. When development of new armaments during the Civil War made the towers obsolete, West Martello was later used for target practice. East Martello had been abandoned after World War I. (Key West Art and Historical Society.)

East Martello was again called into service during World War II, primarily because of its proximity to Meacham Field. While Meacham served as an active blimp base and a training school, Martello provided space for classrooms. Antiaircraft emplacements were set up on top of the fort's citadel, while the grounds offered ample room for barracks and other support buildings. (Key West Art and Historical Society.)

Key Westers turned out in droves for a Navy Day celebration on October 21, 1943. Crowds lined Duval Street in front of buildings decorated with flags and patriotic posters. During World War II, the Navy obviously made a large contribution to the economy of the city. With large ocean-going convoys forming at Key West, the number of men in uniform sometimes surpassed 25,000. While the Marines, Army, and Air Corps all had personnel stationed at Key West, it was definitely a Navy town. Parades served several functions. They boosted civilian morale, showed appreciation for the men and women in uniform, and helped raise funds for the war effort through the sale of war bonds. (Monroe County Public Library.)

Complete with all of the pomp and circumstance of a military function, a change of command ceremony was held for Destroyer Division 601 at the Key West Naval Station. Comprised of both destroyers and destroyer escorts, the division was normally made up of four ships, but at one time, its total strength included 13 ships. During the Cuban missile crisis of October 1962, Destroyer Division 601 played an active role in the blockade of Cuba. (Key West Art and Historical Society.)

In October 1962, the small island of Key West took on the appearance of an armed camp as President John F. Kennedy, Soviet Premier Nikita Khrushchev, and Cuban President Fidel Castro debated the installation of Soviet missiles in Cuba, bringing the world to the brink of war. The 6th Missile Battalion set up radar, antiaircraft missiles, and machine gun emplacements on George Smathers Beach. As tourists strolled Key West's streets, American missiles were pointed toward Cuba, only 90 miles away. (Monroe County Public Library.)

The Navy's crack precision flying team, the Blue Angels, performed at Key West in March 1970. Flying seven McDonnell Douglas F-4J Phantom II aircraft, dual-engine jets they had begun to use the preceding year, the Blue Angels thrilled crowds of spectators. Such aerial demonstrations are designed to assist in recruitment and retention of personnel, as well as to illustrate professional flying skills. (Key West Art and Historical Society.)

Small blimps and their support ships are used to fight aerial and maritime drug trafficking off the coast of Florida. Equipped with airborne radar, the blimps are also used in search-and-rescue missions and to transmit TV Marti to Cuba. Originally a Coast Guard operation, the blimps were transferred to the U.S. Army in 1992. One crewman stated, "We've saved thousands of refugees out here and of course interdicted millions of dollars of drugs." (Monroe County Public Library.)

Fort Jefferson, the "Key to the Mexican Gulf," is located in the string of islands known as the Dry Tortugas, approximately 68 miles west of Key West. Originally designed as part of America's coastal defense system, the fort is now operated by the National Park Service and serves as a prime example of mid-19th-century military construction, a wildlife and marine refuge, and a tourist destination. Although construction began in 1846 and continued for 30 years, the fort was never completed. Situated on approximately ten acres, the six-sided fort was

designed to house a military force of 1,500 men and 450 guns. During the Civil War, the Union-occupied fort played an active role in the blockade of Confederate shipping and served as a federal prison. Dr. Samuel A. Mudd, convicted of conspiracy for treating the injuries of President Lincoln's assassin, John Wilkes Booth, was doubtlessly the fort's most famous prisoner. (Carol Swanick.)

With brick walls rising some 45 feet above a surrounding moat, Fort Jefferson has six bastion towers and a lighthouse. Prior to the outbreak of the Civil War, slave laborers from Key West and St. Augustine did most of the construction until they were gradually replaced by military prisoners. President Franklin D. Roosevelt proclaimed Fort Jefferson a national monument on January 4, 1935. (Monroe County Public Library.)

There are several ways to reach the Dry Tortugas, a group of seven small islands named by Ponce de Leon for the turtles living there. To reach Garden Key, site of Fort Jefferson and the largest of the islands, visitors need to go by seaplane, ferry service, or private boat. The travel is worth the effort. In addition to the fort itself, there is Mother Nature at her best—sandy beaches, unparalleled snorkeling, coral reefs, and abundant wildlife. Approximately 50,000 people visit the Tortugas each year. (Edward Swanick.)

Four

LIVELIHOODS

Since the earliest days of settlement, the waters of the Atlantic Ocean and Gulf of Mexico have provided a livelihood for many Key Westers. Shipping, shipbuilding, fishing, turtling, sponging, salt production, and wrecking were all sea-related businesses that were the life blood of the early Key West economy. A fleet of hundreds of ships manned by sailors from Key West was responsible for the island community once being known as the most affluent city in Florida. An excellent harbor with four entranceways 14 to 33 feet deep allowed ships sailing the trade routes to visit Key West. Ships brought immigrants from the northern states, as well as from the Bahamas and Cuba, forever changing the demographics of the island. The land-based tobacco industry became a major source of wealth because of the influx of Cuban cigar makers. While most of these livelihoods are no longer a part of island life, other activities have taken their place. Crews still fish the surrounding waters for a living, but boats also take millions of visitors sport fishing, diving, snorkeling, and sightseeing. (Key West Art and Historical Society.)

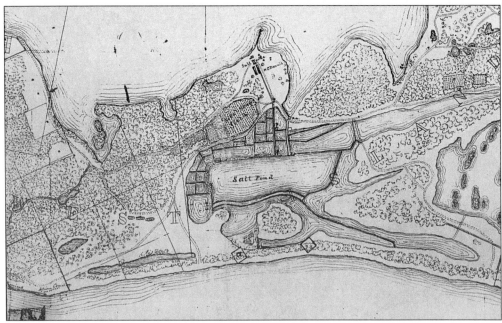

Although early residents hoped that salt would make them rich, success proved elusive. The Civil War halted production; the hurricane of October 19, 1876, destroyed the crop and equipment. Salt ponds on the east end of the island were first put into production in 1830. Floodgates allowed seawater into pans measuring 50 by 100 feet, the water evaporated, and the process was repeated. Eventually the residue crystallized into one-quarter-inch-sized pieces of salt that were raked and bagged for sale. (Monroe County Public Library.)

From its beginning in Key West in the late 1840s, the sponge industry grew at a phenomenal pace. By 1890, Key West had become the sponge capital of the world. Its sponge fishing fleet numbered 350 boats. Nearly 1,300 men were making their living as spongers, harvesting 165 tons of sponges each year. In this photo taken in 1906, the *City of Key West*, a local sponge boat, anchors off the wharf. (Key West Art and Historical Society.)

74

Using a fleet of small boats attached to a mother ship, Key Westers harvested sponges with pronged poles that reached the seabed. In Tarpon Springs, Florida, spongers used an alternative method. Men wearing helmeted diving suits gathered the sponges by hand and carried them to the surface—a quicker, less expensive procedure. In both instances, the sponges were returned to port, spread out to dry, then trimmed, and sold at auction. (Monroe County Public Library.)

Demand for sponges was so great that by the early 1900s, the supply in the Keys began to diminish. By the late 1930s, the local industry was virtually nonexistent. A fungus had devastated the sponge beds, synthetic sponges had been developed, and much of the trade had moved north to Tarpon Springs. A brief resurgence came about during World War II with the military use of sponges as oiled packing material for guns, but the effect was only temporary. (Monroe County Public Library.)

Like many of Key West's early industries, turtling has become a thing of the past. Loggerhead, hawksbill, trunk-back, and green turtles, weighing from 50 to 500 pounds, were caught in the waters near Central America and brought by boat to Key West. Certain varieties were considered to be culinary delicacies, while others were valuable for products made from their shells. (Monroe County Public Library.)

Once in Key West, the live turtles were confined in water-filled pens called kraals or crawls, a name taken from the Dutch word for corrals. An adjacent cannery then butchered and processed the creatures into turtle soup or canned meat. The business ended in the 1970s with the depletion of the turtle population and the enactment of laws protecting the endangered species. (Monroe County Public Library.)

While wrecking was an early industry for Key Westers, most wreckers were also fishermen who sold their live cargoes in Key West and Havana. Salted fish were also shipped to Havana by way of Key West. With the advent of modern transportation and refrigeration, catches could be shipped to more distant points. In recent years, environmental concerns and stricter regulations have further altered the industry. (Library of Congress.)

Key Westers found "pink gold" in 1949 when beds containing vast quantities of large shrimp were discovered near the Dry Tortugas. By the late 1960s, the industry had become a major factor in Key West's economy, filling the waterfront with docks, ice houses, processing plants, and hundreds of shrimp boats. In the early 1990s, however, declining catches combined with increased foreign competition to weaken the market. (Monroe County Public Library.)

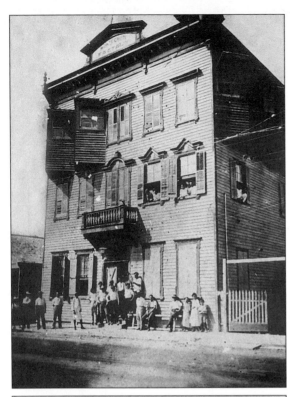

The cigar industry in Key West had a long history since its founding by William Wall in 1831. For the next several decades, as business increased, additional factories were constructed. While the buildings in both of these photographs from the end of the 19th century appear to be the same, they were not. One housed the Monte Cristo cigar factory and the other, the Cortez Cigar Company. As the cigar making industry peaked in the 1880s and early 1890s in Key West, many factories were rapidly constructed in similar styles by the same builders. Utilizing the same design served to minimize costs. (Monroe County Public Library.)

The first large-scale manufacturing of cigars in Key West began in 1867 with Samuel Seidenberg's factory. Thousands of trained cigar makers left the turmoil of the revolution in Cuba for jobs in Key West. Culturally similar to Cuba, the city also offered the perfect climate for making cigars. Heat and humidity were ideal for keeping the tobacco leaf pliable. When most of the wooden factories were destroyed in the 1886 fire, many, including the Havana American Company, were rebuilt of brick. (Monroe County Public Library.)

From the 1870s through 1900, the cigar industry flourished. Factories such as Ruy Lopez provided much of Key West's income. In 1873, there were 15 factories employing 1,200 workers; by 1880, almost 3,000 people were working in 57 factories. The industry reached its peak in 1890 with 129 factories in operation. Thousands of workers produced over 100 million cigars that year. (Monroe County Public Library.)

The first Cuban to own and operate a major Key West cigar factory, Eduardo H. Gato was one of Key West's early success stories. His first factory, which the company quickly outgrew, was located in a building owned by William Curry. Gato eventually purchased land on Simonton Street and built the largest cigar factory in the city. Surrounding the factory, he constructed cottages that he rented to his workers. The enclave became known as Gatoville. (Key West Art and Historical Society.)

Gato's was one of the last large cigar factories to close. With his financial success, he was able to build several luxurious homes for his wife Mercedes and himself. When he returned to Cuba, Gato donated this house to the city as a hospital for the poor. Named Mercedes Hospital, it operated from 1911 until 1944. Constructed of wood with Victorian trimmings, the mansion has also served as a private residence, school, and condominiums. (Monroe County Public Library.)

Cigar makers were highly skilled artisans. With a heavy demand for their services, they were well paid. At the end of the 19th century, cigar makers were earning $15 to $30 per week, while workers in other industries usually made less than $2 per day. The process of making a cigar by hand included stripping, selecting, and packing the tobacco that was then carefully rolled into the finished cigar. Long apprenticeships were frequently required to learn the art of cigar making. (Library of Congress.)

For decades, the cigar factories of Key West dominated the industry. Over the years, workers in the factories of William Wall, Vicente Martinez Ybor, Pincus Pohalski, Ruy Lopez, Samuel Seidenberg, and Eduardo Gato produced hundreds of millions of premium cigars. Such preeminence wasn't to last. Fires, hurricanes, labor conflicts, the relocation of factories and workers to Tampa, and the popularity of cigarettes all led to the decline of Key West as the "Cigar City." By the 1930s, this factory and many others had been abandoned. (Library of Congress.)

By 1934, the Great Depression had devastated Key West to the point that 80 percent of the city's population needed some sort of government financial assistance. Jobs were nonexistent. More than 6,000 residents had moved away; those who remained were barely subsisting. A number of programs were instituted to try to better the situation. As part of the New Deal's relief efforts, the Farm Security Administration sent photographer Arthur Rothstein to Key West to document local conditions. These two images portray a typical Key West scene of a local fisherman with his catch of the day, crawfish (Florida lobster) and conch, and the implements used to obtain them. (Library of Congress.)

Photographed by Rothstein outside of a Key West restaurant, this chalkboard sign listed the specials of the day. With the exception of three items, everything on the menu came from local waters. A bargain by today's standards, the prices seem less favorable when compared to the daily wages of the era, assuming one was lucky enough to be employed. Coupled with the fact that most Key Westers couldn't afford to dine in restaurants during the Depression, business probably wasn't very brisk. For many residents, a steady diet of "grunts and grits" was the norm. When the small local fish were boiled with key limes, onions, green peppers, and seasonings and served over grits, a nutritious and palatable meal resulted. (Library of Congress.)

The situation in Key West was so bad that officials had actually toyed with the idea of relocating the entire population of Key West to Tampa. Julius F. Stone Jr., northeastern director of the Federal Emergency Relief Administration, came to town to set about rectifying the economic situation. A consummate showman, Stone undertook a number of projects to reawaken community spirit, including a two-day festival honoring Cuban patriots in October 1934. (Monroe County Public Library.)

The Federal Emergency Relief Administration (FERA) and the Works Progress Administration (WPA) instituted several programs to help Key Westers gain employment and instill pride. On July 6, 1934, the *Florida Keys Sun* had announced, "Key West to Get New Birth" and "Complete Transformation of the Island into Beautiful Tourist Paradise Planned by FERA." A local performance of *Pirates of Penzance* attended by Harry Hopkins was one of the events designed to publicize Key West. (Monroe County Public Library.)

Julius Stone organized the Key West Volunteer Work Corps, consisting of 4,000 members. They cleaned up the city, painted and remodeled buildings, and planted thousands of coconut palms along the streets of Key West. Not only did planting palm trees provide employment for local residents, the trees added to the tropical ambiance essential to attracting northern tourists. Mayor William Malone and his wife were just two of the local residents involved in the sprucing up of the island. (Monroe County Public Library.)

Palm trees and flowers were just part of Stone's plan. Photographs of thatched-roof cabanas on Rest Beach further promoted the idea of the tropical paradise that awaited visitors. Stone's program worked miracles—unemployment was greatly reduced and during the 1934 winter season, 40,000 tourists visited Key West. The FERA and other relief programs staved off an almost certain financial crisis, helping to beautify Key West and turning it into a vacation destination. (Authors' Collection.)

In 1917, Monroe County issued construction bonds to finance the building of a roadway with connecting bridges paralleling the railroad from Homestead to Key West. Work began in the early 1920s, and finally on January 25, 1928, the new Over-Sea Highway opened for travel. Dressed in silver and lace, the lovely young Rae Louise Russell was designated "Miss Highway 1928" at the festivities. (Shelley Boyd Malone.)

Two stretches of the highway between Lower Matecumbe and No Name Key required a connecting ride by ferryboat. Following the 1935 hurricane, the Florida East Coast Railway made the decision not to rebuild its damaged railroad. Federal and state monies were used to purchase the abandoned railroad right-of-way and bridges; expansion of the highway to Key West began. With great fanfare, the new Overseas Highway opened in 1938. (Library of Congress.)

On February 19, 1939, President Franklin D. Roosevelt and his entourage made the 150-mile trip from Miami to Key West in an open convertible. His trip had several purposes. In part, he wanted to personally inspect the new Overseas Highway that had just opened the preceding year. He also wanted to tour the island that had teetered so close to bankruptcy before being bailed out by the WPA and FERA, two of Roosevelt's New Deal programs. (Key West Art and Historical Society.)

Advertisements touted the new road as an engineering marvel and promised "Off to Sea with No Seasickness." Although narrow bridges had replaced the connecting ferries, the strategic importance of Key West during World War II necessitated still more improvements to the highway. On May 16, 1944, Florida's governor, Spessard L. Holland, proclaimed, "I dedicate this road to the greatness of the Keys." (Authors' Collection.)

As the Overseas Highway made it easier than ever for people to come to the Southernmost City, Key West began to attract less affluent vacationers as well as the wealthy traveler. A forerunner of today's motels, small tourist cabins such as these provided a place for families to stay without an exorbitant expenditure of funds. For those with more money, other alternatives existed. (Monroe County Public Library.)

Opening on New Year's Eve, 1921, Casa Marina was built on an undeveloped section of the island by the Florida East Coast Hotel Company, a subsidiary of Flagler's railroad. Although Flagler always intended to build a luxury hotel at the end of the Florida East Coast Railway's Key West Extension, he died five years before construction began. Final costs for the elegant 200-room resort hotel, advertised as the "most up-to-date in the South," exceeded $350,000. (Monroe County Public Library.)

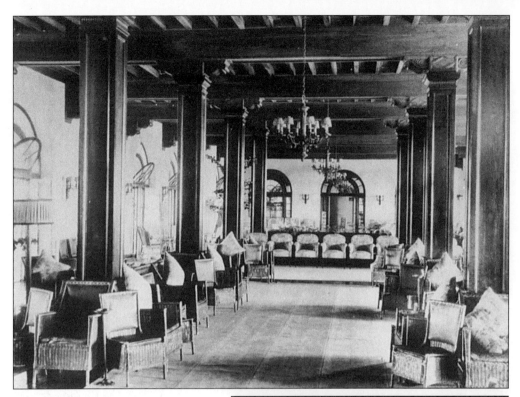

In a similar fashion to most luxury hotels of the era, the public areas of Casa Marina exemplified pre-Depression elegance and sophistication. Guestrooms, on the other hand, varied in both size and amenities. Some included a private bath, while other rooms provided only a sink. Seeing and being seen lay at the heart of the vacation philosophy of the day; wealthy travelers such as the Astors and Vanderbilts spent few waking hours in their rooms. (Monroe County Public Library.)

Using a mixture of cement and native rock, the masonry walls of the hotel ranged in thickness from 22 inches at the base to 12 inches at the roofline. Arched piazzas of the 152-foot-long main building were decorated with tropical plants; wicker chairs provided guests a place from which to gaze upon the ocean. For bathers, a private beach extended along the shoreline. (Monroe County Public Library.)

Recreational opportunities, including fishing, sailing, golf, croquet, and trap shooting, were offered. Guests could play tennis on the Casa Marina's private courts. The "good life" wasn't to last, however. The Depression would close the hotel for several years; periodic financial difficulties would continue. During World War II and again during the missile crisis of 1962, the military occupied the resort. Today, the restored Casa Marina is making an encore appearance as Key West's premier hotel. (Monroe County Public Library.)

For those who couldn't afford the exclusivity of Casa Marina's private beach, there were still opportunities to sunbathe. Public beaches, including one at Fort Taylor and several along the southeastern side of the island, provide spots to swim, windsurf, and snorkel. With the Southernmost House in the background, these sun worshipers are relaxing on South Beach. (Monroe County Public Library.)

Five

A SENSE OF PLACE

Many different things go into creating the atmosphere that draws visitors back to a particular location time after time. The lure may be the people who live there or perhaps it is the activities and things to do. The natural beauty of an area may be the attraction for some, while for others, the beautiful homes and historic structures may be the enticement. In this respect, Key West is more fortunate than many communities, since it has something to offer almost everyone. During the second half of the 20th century, towns across America were caught up in a frenzy of "new is better." Nature came in conflict with the bulldozer. One popular song talked of "paving paradise to put in a parking lot." Important natural resources were lost forever. Where buildings already existed, much of what had made communities special was lost to the demolition that accompanied urban renewal. Fortunately for those who value both environmental treasures and the architectural legacy of the past, Key West to a large degree resisted those impulses. (Key West Art and Historical Society.)

While Key West is world-famous for its sunset celebrations, it is also a place to view a glorious sunrise. One of the best vantage points from which to watch the sun come up over the Atlantic is the White Street Pier. At the entrance to the walkway, inscribed granite panels serve as a memorial to more than 1,000 Key Westers who have died of the AIDS virus. (Authors' Collection.)

Sunrise, sunset, or almost any time in between, birds of all types can be seen throughout the Keys. Perched on pilings, seagulls, brown pelicans, and cormorants watch for passing schools of fish, while keen-eyed osprey dive from above. Careful birdwatchers armed with binoculars and checklists may even spot an occasional roseate spoonbill or white-crowned pigeon in secluded spots on the island. (Monroe County Public Library.)

Sailing is a breeze on the waters surrounding Key West. Winds out of the southeast and deep water both contribute to the joy of boating. For sailboat racers, January is the month to be in Key West, as thousands of sailors arrive on the island to take part in the annual yacht races. Powerboat races take place in May and November, regattas are held throughout the year, and of course, the Christmas holidays feature lighted boat parades. (Monroe County Public Library.)

Catamarans and other small sailboats line Higgs Beach off Atlantic Boulevard. Paddleboats, kayaks, jet skies, floating lounge chairs, rafts, and just about anything else that floats are available to rent at most beaches. Watersports are a major draw for millions of tourists who visit Key West each year. Just as over 100 years ago, the waters surrounding Key West still play a major role in the island's economy. (Authors' Collection.)

Launched off Simonton Beach on April 7, 1939, the *Western Union* was the last tall ship to be constructed in Key West. Used by the Western Union Telegraph Company for more than 30 years to maintain underwater communication cables, the ship logged more than 30,000 miles in the Caribbean and South Atlantic. Today, the *Western Union* is available for day sails, sunset, and starlight cruises, as well as charter trips, giving would-be sailors the chance to heave the lines, raise the sails, or just relive a sailing experience of former days. Retired from active duty in the 1970s, the 130-foot schooner is the officially designated flagship of Key West. (Carol Swanick and Authors' Collection.)

Beginners as well as experts enjoy the excitement of windsurfing in the beautiful clear water surrounding Key West. A combination of surfing and sailing, windsurfing is easy to learn and takes most people only a few hours to master. Each year thousands of windsurfers rig their sails and cruise the waters just off many of Key West's beaches. (Authors' Collection.)

Although they may not have gone sailing or windsurfing, both past and future presidents of the United States, regardless of party affiliation, have loved to visit Key West. Five-star general Dwight D. Eisenhower enjoyed fishing in Key West during the winter of 1946. Six years later, running on his "I like Ike" slogan, Eisenhower would be elected as the 34th president of the United States. (Key West Art and Historical Society.)

95

The Presidential Gates on Whitehead Street were originally intended to be opened only for visits by the President of the United States and other dignitaries. Erected in 1906, the wrought iron gates provide access to the now-decommissioned naval station. President John F. Kennedy was the last president in office to pass through the gates in 1962. No longer a military installation, today the Truman Annex contains upscale residences, as well as the Truman Little White House, opened as a museum in 1991. (Monroe County Public Library.)

All Presidents of the United States have had their private retreats from the overwhelming demands of the office. President Harry Truman's was in Key West. During his presidency, Truman spent 175 days at the remodeled two-story frame residence built in 1890 as housing for the commanding officer at the Naval Station. Christened by the press as Truman's Little White House, the residence has also been visited by Presidents Dwight Eisenhower, John F. Kennedy, and Jimmy Carter. (Monroe County Public Library.)

President Harry Truman and his wife, Bess, loved Key West, returning to the city as often as possible. While at the Little White House, Truman began each day with a morning walk. Time spent at the beach later in the day provided a welcome break from the work that always accompanied presidential vacations. Even after leaving office, the Trumans revisited Key West on several occasions. (Key West Art and Historical Society.)

President John F. Kennedy, like other American leaders, visited Key West on several occasions. During his first trip in 1961, Kennedy and British Prime Minister Harold Macmillan met at the Little White House for talks on Southeast Asia. A year later, following the Cuban missile crisis, Kennedy visited Key West to inspect military forces that had been mobilized in the event military action was taken against Cuba. (Key West Art and Historical Society.)

Chickens, fancy and ordinary, inhabit the yards, both front and back, of many homes and even some businesses. In past years, the fowl provided fresh eggs and occasionally Sunday dinner. Cockfights, although illegal, were also part of the island culture. Today the chickens are just another indication of the unexpected that lurks around any corner in Key West. (Authors' Collection.)

Aureliophiles (cat lovers) will find much to their liking in Key West. Pets of all kinds abound, but cats are among the most numerous, wandering at will throughout the town. Some of the felines have acquired a certain celebrity, however, as well as a place in local lore. At Ernest Hemingway's former residence, cats laze in the sunshine and greet visitors. Among the most distinctive are the polydactyl cats, sporting extra toes on their feet. (Authors' Collection.)

While differing recipes abound, the two common ingredients for that most famous of local desserts—key lime pie—are sweetened condensed milk and key limes. Ordinary green limes won't do; only the tiny yellow key limes grown in South Florida insure an authentic version. For a taste delight, order a piece or an entire pie, but make sure that the filling is yellow. The addition of green food coloring is a definite faux pas. (Authors' Collection.)

Another of promoter Julius Stone's ideas that has retained its popularity is the use of bicycles for transportation. In fact, with parking at a premium, bicycles provide one of the best ways to get around Key West today. The island's flat terrain and total area of only eight square miles make bikes ideal not only for tourists, but also for many residents who use them as their sole mode of transportation. (Authors' Collection.)

Sloppy Joe's Bar, located on the southeast corner of Greene and Duval Streets, is probably the subject of more local lore than any other piece of property in Key West. During Prohibition, the bar's namesake, Joe Russell, provided illegal alcohol, also known as "Hoover Gold," from Cuba and the Bahamas for speakeasies in Key West. Russell, nicknamed Josie or Sloppy Joe, was an ardent fisherman and one of Ernest Hemingway's closest friends. That relationship undoubtedly drew and continues to draw patrons to Sloppy Joe's Bar. Stories abound regarding Hemingway writing books in the back room of the bar. In reality, most of Hemingway's time at Sloppy Joe's was probably spent drinking at the bar. (Monroe County Public Library.)

When the sale and consumption of alcohol again became legal after the repeal of Prohibition in 1933, Joe Russell opened the first Sloppy Joe's in the 400 block of Greene Street. Four years later, he relocated his bar to its present site on Duval Street. The previous location, under different ownership, became the Duval Club and later, Captain Tony's. (Authors' Collection.)

There's hardly a book about Key West, be it fiction or nonfiction, that doesn't feature the Green Parrot, reputedly the "first and last bar on U.S. 1." The building, constructed in the 1890s, is listed on the National Register of Historic Places. Once the site of a morgue, the Brown Derby restaurant, a grocery store, and a point of food and clothing distribution during the Depression, the Green Parrot attracts both local residents and tourists. (Authors' Collection.)

The "Bahama House," Key West, Florida

The oft-photographed Bahama House, with its classic Bahamian-style trademarks of a wrap-around porch and wood-shuttered windows, appears to have been an indigenous part of Key West's architectural landscape. Built of New England white pine, the house was actually constructed in Green Turtle Bay in the Bahamas. Later carefully dismantled board by board, the structure was loaded on a barge and shipped to Key West in 1847 where it was reassembled on its present site. (Authors' Collection.)

This two-story frame house originally constructed by salvager John Geiger opened as the Audubon House and Garden in 1958. Furnished in the style of the 1830s, the museum contains a number of the works of naturalist John James Audubon. Many of the engravings done by Audubon during his visit to Key West in 1832 appeared in his book, *The Birds of America*. Named in honor of Audubon, the house was actually built at least a decade after his visit. (Monroe County Public Library.)

The Ernest Hemingway Home and Museum has a long history. Originally the residence of Asa F. Tift, an early Key West wrecker and wealthy entrepreneur, the house may have been constructed by well-known designer and builder William Kerr. Extensive remodeling following the Hemingways' acquisition of the dwelling in 1931 transformed it into a French Colonial-style building. Among the elements that made the house unique to Key West were its basement and the island's first swimming pool. (Monroe County Public Library.)

Not nearly as elaborate as Ernest Hemingway's home, the house that belonged to Tennessee Williams is a one-story frame structure. To the house, moved to its present location at 1431 Duncan Street some years prior to his purchase, Williams added a writing studio and a swimming pool. A mosaic tile rose tattoo commemorating his play, *The Rose Tattoo*, still decorates the bottom of the pool. (Monroe County Public Library.)

Richard Moore Kemp, a merchant and amateur naturalist for whom the now-endangered Kemp turtle is named, acquired the property at 601 Caroline Street from his family in 1869. Built by John T. Sawyer in 1887-1888 to replace an earlier dwelling that burned in the fire of 1886, the present Kemp House is an excellent example of 19th-century Key West architecture, reflecting a mixture of Classical Revival, Bahamian, and shipbuilding styles. (Monroe County Public Library.)

Photographed in 1967 as part of a Historic American Buildings Survey, the Kemp House bathroom reflected the virtually unaltered condition of the residence. A hand-operated pump carried water from two masonry cisterns located beneath the house to the second-floor bathroom. The interior walls and ceilings of the two-story house consisted of boards just over 3 inches wide that had been left unplastered, a technique known to Key Westers as "sealed walls." (Monroe County Public Library.)

The Kemp House has matching verandas on both the first and second stories of the dwelling. Louvered shutters cover the doors and windows on each floor. For many years, the house was known locally, as well as on myriad postcard views, as the Cypress House. During a recent restoration, analysis of the wood used throughout the structure revealed that the house is in fact built of pine. Treated with a wood sealant but left unpainted, the house has a weathered, silvery appearance. (Monroe County Public Library.)

Just two blocks from Duval Street, Courtney's Place represents the antithesis of hustle and hype. Typical of many of the small enclaves of Conch-style cottages tucked into narrow lanes and alleyways, it offers visitors accommodations in a historic setting. Located on Whitmarsh Lane, named for one of Hemingway's close friends, Courtney's Place makes it easier to understand "old Key West" and gives new meaning to the term "unwind." (Authors' Collection.)

Dating from the 1850s, the Lowe House at 620 Southard Street is one of the finest examples of Bahamian architecture in Key West. Built of pine and Honduran mahogany by John Lowe Jr., a leading sponge merchant and owner of the first electric sawmill in Florida, the house served as a canteen for the USO during World War II and later as a hospital. In this 1912 image, the home was decorated in a most patriotic fashion. (Monroe County Public Library.)

Few houses draw more attention than the one at 1400 Duval Street. Built in 1900 as the home of Judge Jeptha Vining Harris, the Victorian dwelling boasts a number of Queen Anne–style features. Multi-colored in a city where most buildings sport either white or weathered exteriors, the house stands out from all the rest. The house is also well known for another reason. Although no longer true, for many years it was famous as the southernmost house in the United States. (Library of Congress.)

St. Paul's Episcopal Church, in the heart of Old Town, offers a spot for a few moments of quiet reflection amid the boisterous tourist attractions of Duval Street. Built in 1919 on a piece of property donated by John Fleming, this was actually Key West's fourth St. Paul's Church. The original church was constructed in 1838, but destroyed by a hurricane in 1846. The second fell victim to the great fire of 1886, while a hurricane in 1909 demolished the third church. (Authors' Collection.)

Designed by William Kerr in 1875 and demolished in the 1960s, the Convent of Mary Immaculate served as a humanitarian center where the Order of the Sisters of the Holy Names of Jesus and Mary educated Catholic, Spanish-speaking, and black children. During yellow fever outbreaks, the Sisters provided medical care. Turned over to the federal government during the Spanish-American War, the Convent was used as a hospital for many of those brought back from Cuba in 1898. (Key West Art and Historical Society.)

Parades have always been a part of life, and even death, in Key West. In this photograph of the June 1949 funeral of Alfred Skinner, a bartender at Sloppy Joe's, the procession is led by the 17-piece Key West Welters' Cornet Band. Organized in 1874 by Frank Welters, the band was an important part of the cultural life of the community. (Monroe County Public Library.)

The Key West Cemetery is, like the rest of the city, a mixture of elegant and outlandish, staid and quirky. Along with the usual tombstones featuring the requisite urns, cherubs, clasped hands, angels, etc. are the more unique examples of mortuary art. Perhaps indicative of the deceased's interest in aviation, this particular grave is marked by an airplane. (Authors' Collection.)

Six

ARTISTIC AMBIANCE

One of the city's most famous residents was Ernest "Papa" Hemingway. Arriving in 1928 with his second wife, Pauline, the man who has become legendary in Key West fell in love with the town and the town with him. In his writing studio on the second floor of the carriage house in the backyard, Hemingway wrote some of his best literary works, including *A Farewell to Arms*, *Death in the Afternoon*, and *To Have and Have Not*. His years in Key West certainly weren't all work, however. He set up a boxing ring in the backyard and paid local boxers to spar a few rounds with him. He wandered around town in a pair of old cut-off pants, held up with a rope around the waist. Before Pauline ordered the construction of the first swimming pool on the island, he swam each day in the waters near the naval base. Whether soaking up the sunshine on lazy afternoons, or carousing with friends over drinks in local bars, Hemingway fit in perfectly with the island ambiance. (Monroe County Public Library.)

Referring to Key West as "the St. Tropez of the poor," Hemingway's love affair with Key West extended to the surrounding waters and the marine life that lived in them. An avid deep-water fisherman, Hemingway later immortalized his passion for the sea in his award-winning book, *The Old Man and the Sea*. When he and Pauline separated in December 1939, Hemingway left Key West permanently. (Monroe County Public Library.)

Ernest Hemingway spent many hours aboard his boat, *Pilar*. Given the nickname of Hemingway's wife, Pauline, and powered by 75-horsepower Chrysler engines, the 38-foot vessel was built by the Wheeler Shipyard in Brooklyn, New York. Gregorio Fuentes (*Pilar's* skipper), Hemingway, and a host of local residents and visiting celebrities regularly cruised the waters off Key West in search of trophy fish. (Monroe County Public Library.)

Another well-known Pulitzer Prize-winning author Thomas Lanier Williams, better known in literary circles as Tennessee Williams, resided in Key West. First visiting the island in 1941, he quickly became part of the growing group of artists and writers. While living on the sixth floor of the La Concha Hotel in 1946, he worked on *Summer and Smoke*. In 1949, Williams decided to call Key West home permanently, buying a Bahamian-style house at 1431 Duncan Street. *Night of the Iguana* and *Cat on a Hot Tin Roof* were among the works written during the next few years. The Key West Players were the first to perform his play, *Suddenly Last Summer*. When Williams decided to take up painting as an avocation, local artist Henry Faulkner acted as his instructor. Today the Tennessee Williams Fine Arts Center at the Florida Keys Community College on West College Road is named for him. (Monroe County Public Library.)

Pundits claim that there are more writers in Key West per capita than anywhere else in the country. At one time, Pulitzer Prize winner Philip Caputo was one of them. Best known perhaps for his critically acclaimed *A Rumor of War*, Caputo has claimed several Key West properties as home. His former residence at 621 Caroline Street is still known as the Philip Caputo House. (Key West Art and Historical Society.)

Many of Tom McQuane's novels are set in Key West, possibly because they were written in Key West. While living in a house on Ann Street, he worked on *The Bushwhacked Piano*. Living in a Conch-style home on Elizabeth Street, he penned *Panama*. McQuane authored *Ninety-two in the Shade* while living on Von Phister Street. When this novel was made into a movie, McQuane served as its director during filming in the Keys. (Key West Art and Historical Society.)

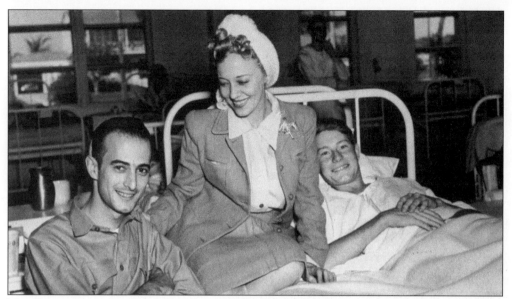

Her famous fans missing, exotic dancer Sally Rand appeared to be the perfect example of propriety as she ministered to the boys at the Naval Hospital during World War II. Rand had been arrested because of her show-stopping act at the Century of Progress Exposition at the Chicago World's Fair in 1933. Concealed by a pair of 7-foot ostrich feather fans and little else, Rand was described as "lewd, lascivious, and degrading to public morals." (Monroe County Public Library.)

The Rose Tattoo, the Academy Award-winning movie version of the play written by Tennessee Williams and starring Burt Lancaster and Anna Magnani, was filmed in Key West in 1955. Among the locations used in the film were St. Paul's Episcopal Church, Casa Marina, and the house next door to Williams' Duncan Street residence. Many local residents found their moment of stardom working as extras in the movie. (Key West Art and Historical Society.)

The Keys have also been the setting for several other motion pictures. Actor Burgess Meredith starred with Margot Kidder in the movie version of Tom McQuane's 1974 novel, *Ninety-two in the Shade*. The story of a young man trying to get started in the fishing business, many of the scenes were filmed in the nearby flats and mangroves as well as at Cow Key Marina. (Key West Art and Historical Society.)

Robert Wagner and Bob Youmans appeared with actors Terry Moore, Peter Graves, and Richard Boone in *Beneath the 12-Mile Reef*. Nominated for an Academy Award for color cinematography, the 1953 film told a classic Romeo and Juliet tale of rivalry between two Key West families engaged in the sponging industry. (Key West Art and Historical Society.)

Cecily Tyson and Geoffrey Holder appeared with Ethel Waters, Coley Wallace, and Richard Ward in *Carib Gold*, a 1955 movie about what else but sunken treasure. Moviemaking in Key West continued with *Escape from Hell Island*, made by a local production company in 1963. *License to Kill* and more recently, *True Lies* were also filmed in the Keys. (Key West Art and Historical Society.)

Lovely young women in swimsuits bedecked with ribbons labeled "Miss Carib Gold" posed at the local premiere of *Carib Gold*. On that evening, a sign hanging at the movie theater read, "W.M. Hill and other LOCAL PEOPLE in a cast also starring Ethel Waters and Corey Wallace." Obviously, folks in Key West had their priorities in the proper order. (Key West Art and Historical Society.)

115

The grandson of cigar makers who moved from Cuba in 1868, nationally renowned folk artist Mario Sanchez was born in Key West in 1908. During the Depression, he began making hand-painted carvings of fish, later expanding his repertoire to renditions of local scenes in the Cuban community of his youth. Sanchez began each work by drawing on a flattened paper bag his proposed design that was then transferred to a wooden board with carbon paper. (Key West Art and Historical Society.)

At his workbench made of pieces of wood attached to the base of his mother's 1930 Singer sewing machine, Mario Sanchez stood for hours carving a rectangular piece of pine, cypress, or cedar. Using three differently sized chisels, a wooden mallet, a broken piece of glass, and a single-edged razor blade, he laboriously chipped away at the board to extract an intricate portrait of bygone days. (Key West Art and Historical Society.)

In his backyard "studio under the trees," Sanchez used dime-store brushes to bring his carvings to life with meticulously applied paints thinned with castor oil. Clear glue added a glistening appearance to windows in his works. Crumbled pieces of limestone from the floor or crushed kitty litter gave the streets the look of the marled thoroughfares of years gone by. (Key West Art and Historical Society.)

Prized by collectors around the world, Mario Sanchez's works are filled with representations of real people and places that once existed in Key West. Even the clouds in his works hold tiny images. Although no longer priced at $1.50 as in the days of the Great Depression, his wood intaglios provide an invaluable look at the past. In his words, "I do this with my heart and my hands." (Key West Art and Historical Society.)

Included with historical exhibits and the works of Mario Sanchez at the East Martello Museum and Gallery are the sculptures of Stanley Papio. Pictured here in 1982 with a work titled "Las Vegas Model," the artist frequently came in conflict with both neighbors and zoning regulations as he created his welded sculptures from car parts, discarded scrap metal, and assorted junk in the yard of his Key Largo residence. (Key West Art and Historical Society.)

Three galleries share space in a former Firestone Tire Company building on Duval Street. Parked in front is an eye-catching piece of art—a 1971 Alfa Romeo that has been completely covered with thousands of pieces of irregularly shaped glass and tile. Sporting pink sidewall tires covered with blue and yellow tiles, artist Lenny Addrisio's creation is definitely designed to stop strolling pedestrians in their tracks. (Authors' Collection.)

Another more mobile version of the same concept can be spotted at various locations on the streets around town. Designed by artist Rick Worth, a vintage Volkswagen beetle with a license plate reading "ART CAR" has been covered with a colorful glass and tile mosaic of marine life. Poised above the roof is a swimming dog. (Authors' Collection.)

Many of the Key West inns and guesthouses were originally built as private homes for the island's wealthiest inhabitants. The Red Rooster Inn on Truman Avenue began life as a mansion constructed in 1870, later provided housing for military personnel, and today offers accommodations to visitors. Located on the second floor veranda, this giant rooster adds a thematic note to the decor. (Authors' Collection.)

Is it or is it not the largest conch in the world? You be the judge. This gigantic reproduction of a conch, the symbol of Key West, sits in front of Key West High School at 2100 Flagler Avenue. Welded from scrap metal in 1986 by the high school shop class under the supervision of George Carey Jr., the conch stands nearly 19 feet high and is 14 feet wide. Its weight is described as "heavy." Visitors should also be on the lookout for a ferocious tiger stalking the grounds of the Glynn Archer Junior High School at the corner of White and United Streets. Another work by the talented George Carey and his students, the metal sculpture mascot adorns the grounds of the former Monroe County High School. (Authors' Collection.)

Eccentric individuals have always been a part of the Key West scene. This photo, taken in 1970, pictures a local gentleman popularly known as "Iguana Man." His rather ferocious looking iguana was reputed to be 18 years old at the time. The age of the smaller lizard on its back is unknown. (Key West Art and Historical Society.)

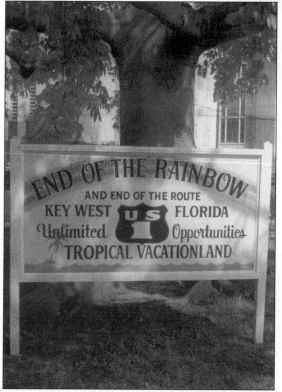

One of the most photographed landmarks in Key West is the End of the Rainbow sign on the grounds of the Monroe County Courthouse. Located on Whitehead Street, this spot is where it all ends—or perhaps more appropriately, begins—the 2,209-mile stretch of U.S. Highway 1 running north from Key West to Maine. You too can become part of history—one of the millions who either have been or will be photographed here. (Authors' Collection.)

Pictured here with Betty Williams, an editor for the Key West *Citizen*, Jimmy Buffett, singer, songwriter, and local legend, spent most of the 1970s in Key West. Recording the first of his best-selling albums in 1973, he achieved success with numerous songs based upon his version of the good life in Key West. An ardent environmentalist, Jimmy Buffett is particularly active in the fight to save the endangered manatee. (Monroe County Public Library.)

There is no better place for Parrotheads, those devotees of Jimmy Buffett, than their Mecca—Key West, the capital of which is of course Margaritaville, Buffett's restaurant and bar on Duval Street. Each October, Parrotheads come from all over the world to celebrate their shared interest in the singer's music and the lifestyle represented in his songs. "Cheeseburgers in Paradise," margaritas, Hawaiian shirts, tie-dyed clothing, and other flavors of the 1960s add to the color. (Everett Glover.)

CONCH REPUBLIC

We Seceded Where Others Failed

PASSPORTS

One of the best examples of the independence of spirit that exemplifies Key West is the story of the secession of the Florida Keys from the United States. On April 23, 1982, the U.S. Border Patrol road-blocked the highway from the Keys to the mainland and searched vehicles traveling in both directions for illegal aliens and drugs. The immediate result was a monumental traffic jam and lots of bad press. Local officials and businessmen turned the situation into a public relations dream by declaring the independence of the Keys from America. At Mallory Square, the Keys seceded, a single shot was fired into the air, and war was declared, quickly followed by a surrender and application for foreign aid. Today the Conch Republic Independence Day Celebration, commemorated annually each April, relives that occasion with flags, passports, officials, and all kinds of festivities. (Peter Anderson.)

Once a year, visitors to Key West might think that they were seeing ghosts or at least reincarnations of that famous resident of bygone days, Ernest Hemingway. It's not really true, however, but rather the annual celebration of Hemingway Days, held the week surrounding July 21, the author's birthday. Festival activities include short story contests, sporting events, and the most famous event, the Hemingway Look-alike competition at Sloppy Joe's Bar. (Courtney's Place.)

Judging from this photograph, costume occasions such as Mardi Gras, Halloween, and Fantasy Fest aren't just a recent phenomenon. One can only speculate about an occasion that would inspire attendance by a would-be Pancho Villa, a circus ringmaster, a clown, a Scotsman, an Argentinean cowboy, and a George Washington look-alike. (Key West Art and Historical Society.)

While every month of the year is filled with special events, October features perhaps the most famous happening of all. Fantasy Fest, Key West's version of Marti Gras, is a ten-day party attended by more than 50,000 visitors from all over the world. All kinds of activities, both family- and adult-oriented take place, including street fairs, pet masquerades, toga parties, and of course, parades. Held on the last Saturday evening of October, the culmination of the celebration is the Twilight Fantasy Parade, featuring revelers in costumes ranging from the outstanding to the outrageous. In an uncertain world, Fantasy Fest can be counted upon to outdo itself year after year. (Courtney's Place.)

Another of the special events that take place throughout the year is a celebration called Old Island Days. Various activities commemorating Key West's island culture include an art show, a conch blowing contest, a ceremonial blessing of the fishing fleet, and ethnic food festivals. Observed by a crowd of enthusiastic spectators, these gentlemen are competing in a limbo contest. (Monroe County Public Library.)

On the portion of the Key West waterfront known today as Mallory Square, Lieutenant Matthew Perry, commander of the U.S.S. *Shark*, took possession of Key West in 1822 as part of the territory ceded to the United States by Spain. He also named Key West Thompson's Island in honor of the Secretary of the Navy; fortunately, the name didn't last. Today, Mallory Square is famous for its sunset celebrations and street-carnival atmosphere. The only time to see the area without people is early in the morning. (Authors' Collection.)

Bagpipers, jugglers, musicians, acrobats, stilt-walkers, and mimes all earn their livings by competing for donations from the throngs who saunter down Duval Street to end their walk at Mallory Square just in time to participate in the sunset festivities. Poised on her pedestal, this young woman resists all blandishments to unfreeze her statue-like demeanor. (Authors' Collection.)

One of the most popular acts at the sunset celebration is that of the "cat man," professionally known as Dominique and his Flying House Cats. A presence on the sunset celebration scene since 1984, Dominique Lefort stages a show that culminates with one of his carefully trained housecats jumping through a flaming hoop—much to the apparent amazement of all concerned. (Authors' Collection.)

The situation at the sunset celebration is much the same as in a movie theater—after the previews and advertisements, the feature begins. When all of the entertainers have been seen, the margaritas drunk, and the conch fritters and shrimp cocktails consumed, the main attraction starts. As the glowing round ball of flame that is the setting sun goes down beyond the horizon, the audience breaks into cheers and a thunderous ovation. Another glorious day in the Southernmost City has ended; the nighttime revelry is about to begin. (Monroe County Public Library and Everett Glover.)